EXPLORATORIUM

A SEARCH & COLOUR MISSION

LOM
ART

WELCOME TO MY INFINITE UNIVERSE...

Explore the farthest reaches of my crazy doodle universe, packed with weird and wonderful landscapes and bizarre creatures called Misfits. From spectacular underwater worlds to fantastical cityscapes, each out-of-this-world scene comes straight from my wildest imagination.

Your task is to travel from scene to scene to find a collection of Misfits. They are listed and shown. Some are good creatures, some are bad, but all have a sense of mischief that makes them very tricky to track down!

There will be characters hiding in each intricately-detailed picture. It's truly tricky to spot them. Their descriptions will give you hints on where they are. Remember, they are masters of disguise, so you might only catch a glinting eye, a distinctive tooth or the glimpse of a smile. Follow the clues, then colour the creatures as you find them so they don't disappear again.

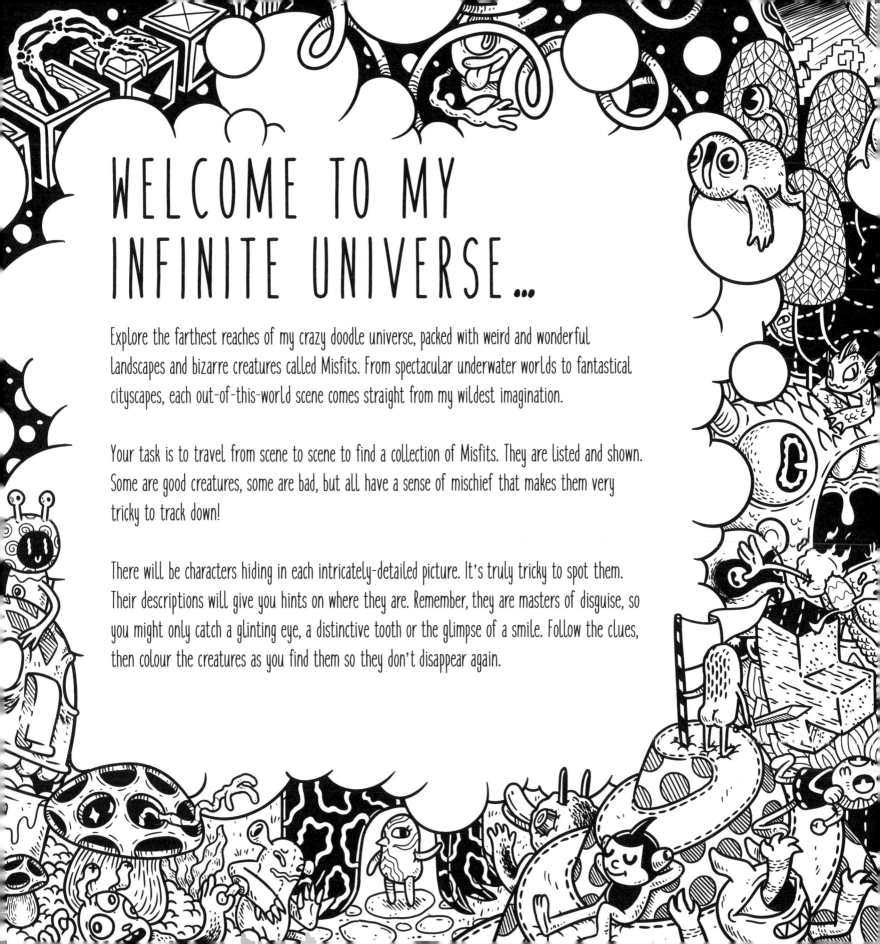

This is Astros. An earthling on a mission to explore the doodle universe, he is lost in one scene — try to hunt him down before the Misfits capture him and put an end to his explorations.

The objects below are hidden throughout the book — pay close attention and count how many times they appear and write your totals here.

🌰 = ☐   🥛 = ☐   🎲 = ☐   🍪 = ☐

☕ = ☐   🌟 = ☐   ✏️ = ☐

Don't panic! If your brain begins to boggle, all the answers are in the back of the book.

@leimelendres

ALIEN INVASION

A UFO-load of Misfit daredevils have landed with one aim — to take over the planet and turn everyone into oddities like them. Can you use the clues to seek out the following Misfits and colour them in to stop their mission and save the world?

BURGLARRY A sticky-fingered rogue with a penchant for breaking and entering, Burglarry has got a head for heights — he specializes in scaling walls and climbing trees and practises his talent whenever and wherever he can.

SHAKEY A mass of contradictions, Shakey is a shy Misfit but hates to be left alone. She sticks close to non-Misfit characters, hitching a ride with them if she gets the chance.

KAPPAH A bit of an outcast, Kappah often finds himself on the outside looking in, observing the crowds. His favourite viewpoints are high up in the trees, so he can watch people without being spotted.

CHIDOG Greedy, cute and bold, Chidog's trick is befriending picnickers in the park so he can steal their food. He perches up high so he can swoop on his favourite snacks.

ORION One of the last to leave the spaceship, Orion is a happy chap who is keen to make friends with both Misfits and earthlings.

CRAZY TOWN

This is no ordinary city — it's a mixed-up metropolis harbouring gangs of madcap Misfits. Scour the mean streets and soaring skyscrapers to hunt down the characters listed below and highlight them before they take over the town. Don't forget, there are clues in their descriptions.

BROW An awkward loner whose goal is to overcome his shyness once and for all, Brow spends his days visiting other Misfits in their homes in a bid to hone his conversational skills.

DULBEE A genius baby Misfit, Dulbee loves watching watersports, especially river rafting.

PYRHEAD On a mission to search for his missing eye, Pyrhead's distinctive pyramid head should mean that he's a doddle to find but he has a knack of evading even the most determined of Misfit hunters.

FRIBLE A true food lover, Frible is allergic to the kitchen so spends all of her time and money in and around the cafes of Crazy Town.

FOOD FIGHT

There's no such thing as a quiet lunch in this crazy cafeteria — but is the food fight a diversionary tactic so you can't find these mischievous Misfits? Dodge the flying foodstuffs and spot the characters below.

LICKIE Boisterous and a know-it-all, Lickie swaggers about like he owns the place. He's prone to starting trouble then ducking under the table, leaving others to take the blame.

CLOFOAM A timid and non-confrontational character, Clofoam hates arguments and shies away from any sort of conflict, particularly of the messy or food-based variety.

BEESTLE Beestle lurks in corners waiting for people to notice her. In fact, this attention-seeking Misfit laps up any sort of attention.

CHELIO At home in the kitchen, Chelio loves Misfits who enjoy her food but she hates waste — seeing her tasty dishes thrown around in food fights makes her very angry.

STRIO Only going to the cafeteria to meet up with other Misfits, Strio hates the thought of eating in front of others, so she hides until she misses her place in the queue.

TIME TRAVELLER

This mixed bag of oddities have travelled from different eras to gather in the only place they feel at home — a land where time has no meaning. Hunt them down using the clues below.

SPIFF An enthusiastic time tourist, Spiff sticks close to the time machine whenever he fancies a change of scenery.

NINBOY Blinded in a duel, centuries ago, Ninboy uses his fencing sword to feel his way to the smallest and most secluded hiding places, where he can hunker down in safety.

CAVIAR The most ancient oddity ever known, Caviar was responsible for the first cave paintings and now claims to have invented art.

BLINTY Nobody is exactly sure where Blinty came from or how long he has been hanging around, but they know he prefers the company of bigger, stronger tree-loving Misfits.

CANDY LAND

This collection of oddities look sweet enough to eat, but don't be fooled — they will leave a bad taste in your mouth if you don't track them down. Explore the ice-cream mountains and cupcake-covered pathways to discover a delicious secret world.

DIABITO Like all of the Misfits in Candy Land, Diabito loves everything sweet. He is particularly drawn to anything fluffy, so try to find him before he devours the candyfloss characters.

CREAMDRU Prone to using too much icing on his hair, you'll recognise Creamdru by his big, sticky quiff. He's obsessed with eating lollipops for every meal — the bigger the better.

FLAKE A discerning cake expert who has travelled the universe on a sponge-tasting mission, she will now only eat the biggest tiered sponge cakes she can find.

MARSH They say you are what you eat, and Marsh got her nickname because she is always hanging out around the mallow trees, sneaking a taste whenever she can.

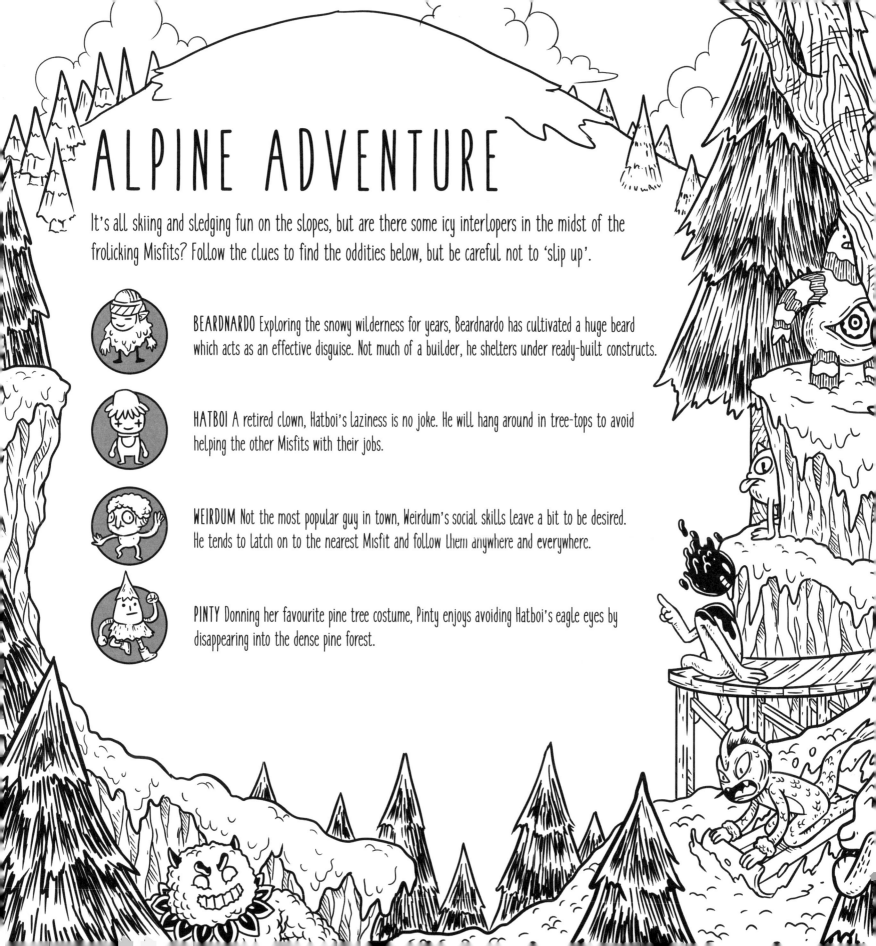

ALPINE ADVENTURE

It's all skiing and sledging fun on the slopes, but are there some icy interlopers in the midst of the frolicking Misfits? Follow the clues to find the oddities below, but be careful not to 'slip up'.

BEARDNARDO Exploring the snowy wilderness for years, Beardnardo has cultivated a huge beard which acts as an effective disguise. Not much of a builder, he shelters under ready-built constructs.

HATBOI A retired clown, Hatboi's laziness is no joke. He will hang around in tree-tops to avoid helping the other Misfits with their jobs.

WEIRDUM Not the most popular guy in town, Weirdum's social skills leave a bit to be desired. He tends to latch on to the nearest Misfit and follow them anywhere and everywhere.

PINTY Donning her favourite pine tree costume, Pinty enjoys avoiding Hatboi's eagle eyes by disappearing into the dense pine forest.

CIRCUS

It's mayhem in the Big Top and these crazy characters are taking advantage by hiding in the crowds.
Keep your eyes peeled to pick them out or you'll be jumping through hoops to find them.

QUIDO Super-smart and very adventurous, Quido is a part-time physics professor and full-time funseeker. He uses his super physics knowledge to help him perform in the ring.

PICAWHALE A magnet for trouble, Picawhale always seems to fall in with the wrong crowd. His new best friend is the circus elephant.

EYEOPTOPUS Unlike some of his more acrobatic associates, this Misfit doesn't have a head for the spotlight— he prefers to blend in at the back of the crowd.

LIPPA Daredevils beware! Lippa is drawn to adrenaline junkies and will do anything it takes to befriend them — she can often be found hanging out ringside, waiting for the acrobats to swing by.

FRIGHT NIGHT

Anyone could be a Misfit in their freaky festive costumes, so it's extra-hard to identify the real horrors in this spooky scene. Look closely, though, because these rogues are definitely more trick than treat.

HALLOWORM A bit of a slippery customer, Halloworm's favourite game is hide and seek, especially on Halloween night when there are lots of decorations to camouflage him.

FREEBO A good friend of Halloworm, Freebo is an expert at hiding in bushes, making him a tough hide-and-seek opponent. Can you find him before Halloworm seeks him out?

SPIKES A magpie-like Misfit who is drawn to bright and shiny objects, Spikes spends her time hunting for coins on the ground and in other Misfits' gardens.

GRUMPBAT Not as miserable as he looks, Grumpbat is actually a sweet and caring Misfit who has a penchant for climbing roofs to keep an eye on the action on the ground. He makes sure Spikes' pilfering doesn't get her into trouble.

FUTURE CITY

These Misfits inhabit a world where nothing is impossible—from flying cars to invisibility shields, self-propelled spacesuits to fly-thru burger joints. It would be easy to get lost here, so take care as you hunt the characters below.

BLOBBY A visitor to Future City, Blobby is just passing through as part of his infinite exploration — he's not used to crowds so be careful on the stairs, he's likely to get under your feet.

TRIX The worst prankster of all Misfits, EVER, Trix is dangerously mischievous and loves tampering with engines to cause 'hilarious' accidents.

HAYBIRD A winged but flightless Misfit, Haybird loves watching the flying cars and dreaming of what could have been. If only he was blessed with working wings.

ROBO BAIT An experiment gone wrong from the Robo Lab, Robo Bait is enjoying her new freedom catching fish in Future City with her new cuddly bear friend.

FLEETROW A turbocharged cyborg Misfit with a daredevil streak, Fleetrow loves racing flying cars through the tunnels of Future City.

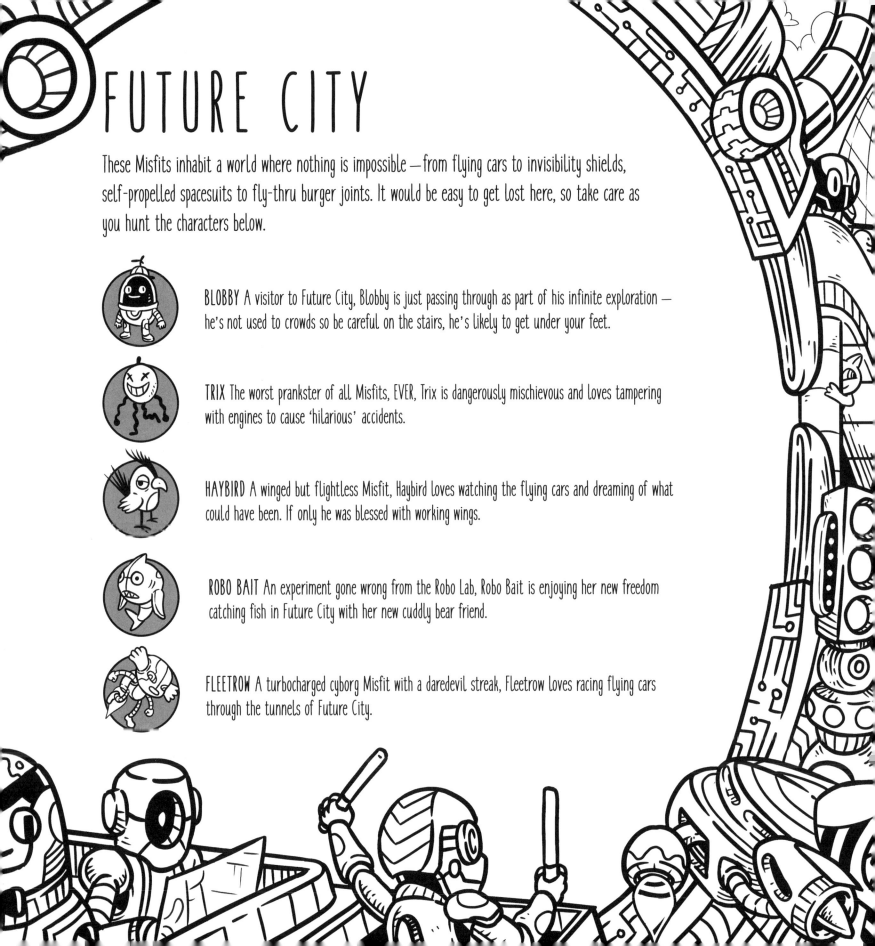

FAIRGROUND

Roll up, roll up! This fantastical fairground is home to the biggest, scariest rides along with a collection of the freakiest oddities you are likely to find. Follow the clues to track them down.

DOWNER A timid Misfit who finds it hard to make friends, Downer lurks backstage hoping someone will see through his shyness and bring him out of his shell.

JELLYBEAR An unusual jellyfish and bear hybrid, Jellybear loves to dance and has a famously unique sense of rhythm.

STYRONE An adrenaline junkie who travels the universe in search of the ultimate thrill, Styrone is always first in line for the biggest rollercoaster at the fair.

CLOUDY Appearances can be deceptive — Cloudy may look soft and cuddly but she's actually made of solid steel and passes her time watching shoot 'em up games.

SCIENCE LAB

It's all mad scientists and mixed-up experiments in this loopy lab of ludicrous oddities. It looks like you have stumbled across some secret testing. Find these bonkers boffins and stop their crazy tests.

CRITTER A subject of a science experiment, Critter used to love playing with coral and seaweed in his underwater home, but now all he has to keep him amused are the wires and cables from the lab machinery.

FLAIRT Proud to be the head assistant for the top scientist at the lab, Flairt has one major grumble about her position — she has to stick close to her braniac boss at all times.

CLOWREED The top scientist at the lab has a pet dog, who has a toy clown — this is Clowreed. He was brought to life with a potion but he has to hide under lab equipment to avoid further experimentation.

SPIKEEY An expert mixologist, Spikeey's job is to make special blends of the lab's most secret ingredients for the scientists to test on the Misfits they capture.

SUPER SAFARI

It's not just animals that are the 'mane' attraction on this super safari. A collection of weird and wonderful creatures are lurking in the places you least expect. You won't need your binoculars but you might need some clever clues to find their hiding places.

TREENJA Treenja pretends that she's not scared of wild animals but she is often found sticking suspiciously close to the bigger, scarier Misfits.

BUMPY Although he enjoys taking the opportunity for a cooling dip in the local watering hole, Bumpy gets a bit self-conscious when other Misfits are around. He prefers to hide out until he can have a solitary swim.

ESPIRAL An undercover scientist, Espiral has been shipped in to study the resident Misfits but he pretends he is collecting data about safari animals.

CRUTS A fascination with plants, trees and anything that grows means Cruts is often found at ground level, studying the soil for new species of plants and flowers.

UNICRU A Misfit of small stature, Unicru is fascinated by the bigger safari creatures and hangs around them hoping their size will rub off on him.

NORTH POLE

Brrrrr! Take inspiration from these mad meteorologists and wrap up warm at the weather station — there's work to be done. Join these Misfits on their mission to control the whole world's seasons.

PUMPAO Chief weatherman Pumpao is never off-duty, spending most of his time in the weather tower obsessively recording every blip and blizzard.

BLIZARO Put together from spare parts, Blizaro is the closest thing to a real-life robot that's ever existed. His main role is to help to maintain the delicate and complicated equipment.

STARCHY Amateur astronomer Starchy sleeps all day and stargazes all night. He has a crick in his neck from craning to spot his favourite constellations from the ground.

BUNDIT Party animal Bundit is also a night owl, but clashes with Starchy who accuses him of disturbing his peace and quiet and distracting him from his hobby.

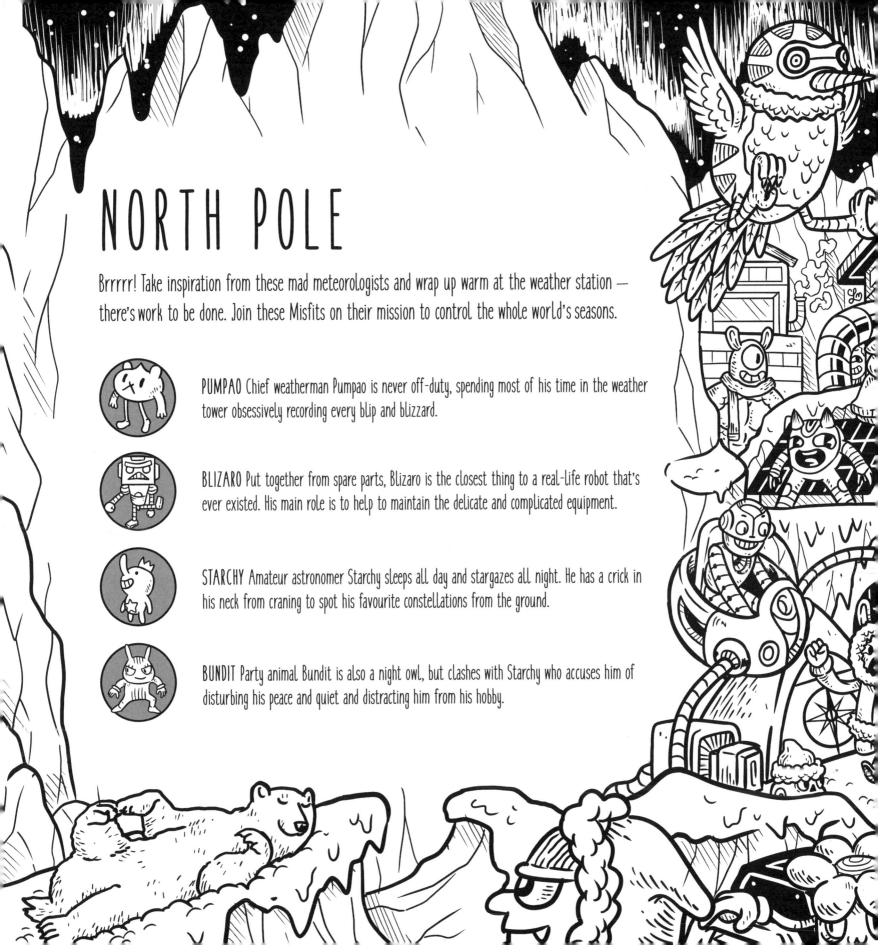

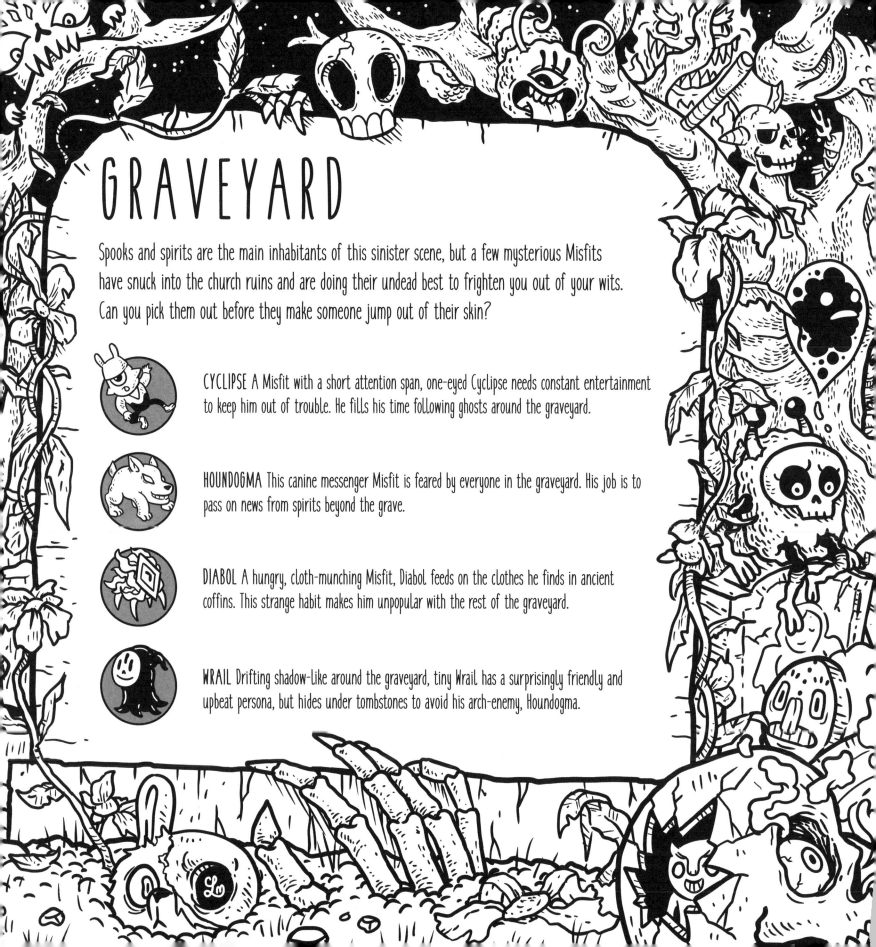

GRAVEYARD

Spooks and spirits are the main inhabitants of this sinister scene, but a few mysterious Misfits have snuck into the church ruins and are doing their undead best to frighten you out of your wits. Can you pick them out before they make someone jump out of their skin?

CYCLIPSE A Misfit with a short attention span, one-eyed Cyclipse needs constant entertainment to keep him out of trouble. He fills his time following ghosts around the graveyard.

HOUNDOGMA This canine messenger Misfit is feared by everyone in the graveyard. His job is to pass on news from spirits beyond the grave.

DIABOL A hungry, cloth-munching Misfit, Diabol feeds on the clothes he finds in ancient coffins. This strange habit makes him unpopular with the rest of the graveyard.

WRAIL Drifting shadow-like around the graveyard, tiny Wrail has a surprisingly friendly and upbeat persona, but hides under tombstones to avoid his arch-enemy, Houndogma.

UNDER THE SEA

A vast collection of otherworldly characters are lurking in the dark, mysterious depths. The shadowy seabed can't hide them for long, though, especially not with an intrepid explorer like you on the case.

CURLY An aquatic enthusiast with a thirst for knowledge, Curly is happiest when he's keeping a low profile, searching for different kinds of coral and seaweed on the seabed.

BISH This confused creature doesn't know if he's a fish or a bird, but he does know he's got a temper and is always ready to fight anyone who makes fun of his uncertainty.

BLUNNY A solitary oddity, Blunny will go to any lengths to avoid interacting with others, making her hiding place in the darkest corner she can find.

U.F.OCEAN A visitor to this underwater habitat, U.F.Ocean is searching HIGH and low for new species to capture and take back to his own planet.

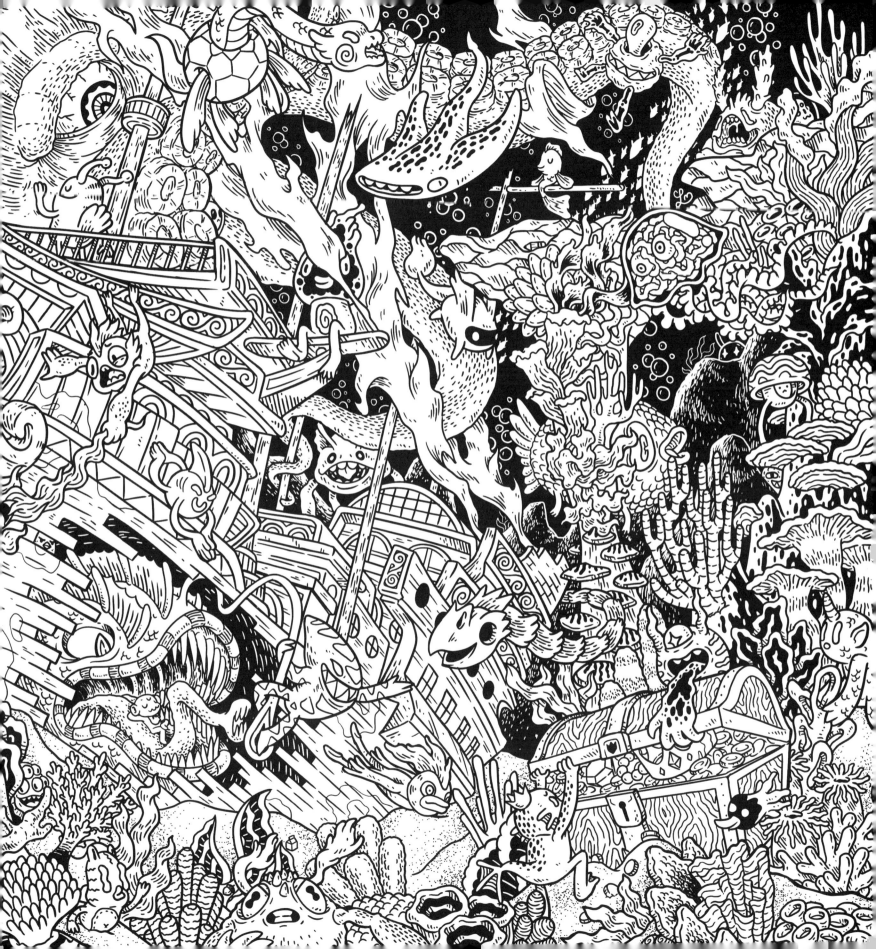

ROBOT FACTORY

Working day and night to produce hundreds of robots, there are bound to be some rejects that slip through the net. Now the rejects are running riot through the factory, causing chaos at every turn.

SHADY A big fan of playing hide and seek, Shady's favourite trick is sticking close to the shadows of the other Misfits — this means he stays out of trouble because everyone else gets blamed for his antics.

ROBEAR A rosy-cheeked rogue, Robear is in charge of quality control at the robot factory but his bossy ways mean he is unpopular with the other Misfits.

SMUGG Sneaky and with a wicked sense of humour, Smugg has been known to loiter under the conveyor belt, waiting to scare the workers.

BIBBO A happy-go-lucky Misfit, Bibbo tries to cheer up the factory workers on the production line who are overworked, underpaid and at the mercy of rampaging robot rejects.

HORNABLIS Likes to fight the stifling factory conditions by chilling out next to the biggest fan he can find.

RIVER RAMPAGE

These rafting rascals are escaping down-river. The lush undergrowth provides the perfect hiding place for those left behind, but follow the clues to lead our elusive friends out of their hiding places.

CHIP A small, bird-like Misfit with a big attitude problem, Chip says she prefers to hang out alone in the treetops, but is really paranoid that the other Misfits avoid her, rather than the other way around.

TWOOTH A good friend to all Misfits, Twooth makes it his mission to cheer up anyone who is feeling sad or lonely. He is searching behind rocks to find Chip so he can persuade her to join in with the rest of the group.

DOLPHY The river rapids are the perfect environment for Dolphy, a world-class diver who loves to challenge herself in the rapids close to her jungle hut home. She likes to wait on the bank to dive in.

CREADO A melting Misfit with a dangerous streak, Creado will watch as swimmers take on the rapids and laugh when they get into trouble, only stepping in to help rescue them at the last second.

SKATE PARK

Ollies, noseslides and frontsides are the only way to get these cool characters to pay you attention — luckily you can spy on them without being spotted.

TRITU A complete show-off by nature, Tritu is obsessed with exotic pets and loves the attention his collection brings him as he parades them around the park.

BLOC Always searching for a bit of zen-like calm as he looks down on this fast and furious environment, Bloc hides out behind the halfpipe.

PUSHIE Shy and subdued, Pushie likes to watch the action from as cosy a spot as he can find, often bedding down in the foam pit.

BUN BUN An ex-skate champ who lost his skateboard collection in a monster attack, Bun Bun now sulks by the ramps waiting for someone to lend him their board.

FOREST HUNT

Deep in the mystical forest, weird creatures lurk in the trees, strange beasts hide in the undergrowth and you might catch sight of a one-eyed Cyclops or a zombie in disguise as you explore this unknown territory. Hunt the characters below and colour them so they can't escape.

ROBO BOY Robot experiment escapee Robo Boy is doing his best to stay undercover. He's on the run from both the Robo Lab and Tommy Kid and he's a master of disguise, but it will take more than a HIGH-ding place to throw you off the scent.

SILENT STITCH An ogre of few words, Stitch uses his silence to his advantage when skulking halfway up trees. You might feel the burn of his one-eyed unblinking gaze as he watches you from his favourite spot.

TOMMY KID Not quite as innocent as he looks, Tommy Kid is a rebel with a cause — to track down Robo Boy, take him back to the lab and claim his bounty.

TALL HAT Tall Hat is welded to his favourite accessory, which should make spotting him in the bushes a breeze. But he's not as silly as he looks and there are plenty of hiding places for this fashionable beast who just wants to be left alone.

BIRDBIT Embarassed by his lack of flying ability, Birdbit is often found skulking in the bushes to avoid run-ins with more adept fliers.

HAUNTED HOUSE

These ghoulish Misfits are on the terror trail, hiding in the cobwebs and spooking anyone who dares to venture inside. Search them out before they can give anyone else a scare ... if you dare!

LEAKID Unusually, Leakid's body is made entirely of liquid. He wears a special suit so he doesn't spill through the cracks in the grand staircase and disappear.

STICKBOY Inspired by ninja drawings, Stickboy is a master of covert operations — creeping around, showing up in the most unlikely of places and disappearing just as quickly. Will you be the one to catch this slippery customer before he disappears?

EYELIEN Brave and bold, Eyelien doesn't scare easily. There isn't a place in the haunted house that is out of bounds and he is happy to hang out at great heights.

FOOTLESS He may look freaky, but Footless is a cheerful character who doesn't let his missing limbs stop him from having fun. His favourite hobby is climbing, and there are plenty of places to clamber about in this dilapidated dwelling.

INFINITY AND BEYOND...

Travel to the outer reaches of the unknown universe on the hunt for aliens, Misfits and oddities, who are travelling on a spacecraft 'borrowed' from a disused space station. Hunt down these elusive characters before they rocket into outer space forever.

SPACE GHOST A loner who avoids the company of other Misfits like the plague. Space Ghost hangs out alone at the end of the laserbeam.

NOODLE MASK Noodle is obsessed with all things explosive. His habit of letting off fireworks everywhere he goes might help illuminate him in the dark.

TRIO EYE A lively, laidback character, Trio's motto is 'don't worry, be happy' — and he is! Mostly when he's floating through the night sky.

MINI TIKI Not a native of the Misfit world he inhabits, Mini Tiki hitched a ride on the borrowed spacecraft and has been travelling with the crew ever since — can you find him before the others realise?

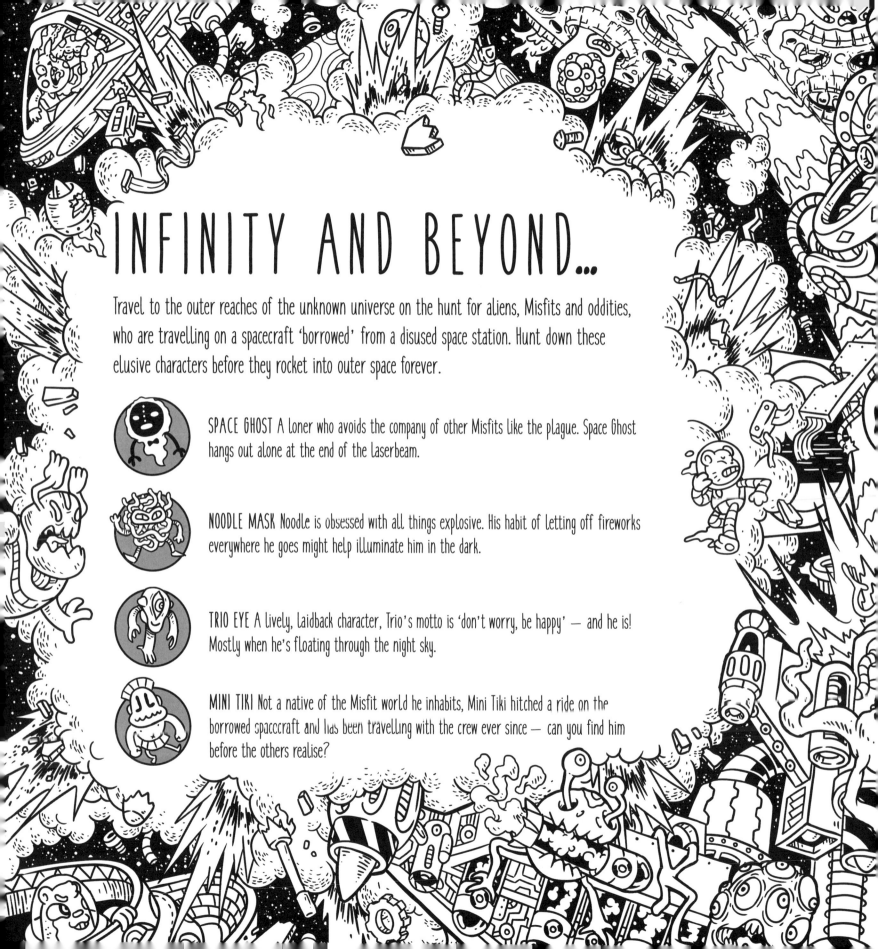

VOLCANO

It might look dangerous but this explosive scene is home to some of the most intrepid adventurers in the Misfit universe. See if you can spot the explorers below by following the clues.

 SCREEMY A fearless thrillseeker with one impossible challenge on his mind, Screemy dreams of scaling the volcano and then sliding down the slopes like it's a helter-skelter.

 LIZARVE Living at the foot of a volcano might seem like a dangerous choice, but Lizarve is fearless — mostly because she knows her fireproof outer layers will protect her.

 PETAR Avoiding the heat of the bubbling lava is Petar's main occupation — she prefers to hang out near the mountains waiting for something awesome to happen.

 **BIKI** A Misfit with a weird attraction to slimy, slippery and gooey stuff, Biki loves the bubbling molten lava from the volcano. But she tends to watch it from behind a tree.

RAINFOREST

This dense and humid jungle is alive with freaky creatures and bizarre beasts. From the forest floor to the highest treetops, every inch is teeming with characters to observe. Can you pick out the ones below?

AFROCURL A happy-go-lucky character who loves to keep active, Afrocurl particularly enjoys life in the tree tops, looking down on the rainforest canopy.

DEVIN Like Afrocurl, Devin is often found hiding out at the top of the tallest trees in the rainforest. But unlike Afrocurl, he is mainly keen to avoid the company of other, more sociable characters.

BUFFBEAR With his over-developed physique and inferiority complex, Buffbear is a vain Misfit who is obsessed with eavesdropping behind trees to make sure others aren't talking about him behind his back. Pick him out and stop him spying.

TRI-VADER A nature-loving ninja, Tri-vader is fascinated by anything to do with tree-dwelling insects. Luckily there are plenty of unusual types in the rainforest for him to study.

POOL PARTY

The music is loud, the drinks are flowing and the vibes are cool at this tropical pool party. These Misfits have snuck away for some down time but the clues below will help you track them down.

TRIDENT Keen to extend his fitness routine beyond karate, Trident has recently taken up swimming but is still splashing around in the shallow end.

THREEBIRD Less boisterous than some of the other Misfits at the party, Threebird is nervous to join in the fun and is scared to try out the slide, despite Comobot's encouragement.

FASTATA Always the first on the dancefloor and the last to leave, Fastata is a real party animal and a pool party is his favourite kind. He loves to play games with beach balls.

NAGGOAT The unofficial DJ at every party, Naggoat always turns the music up to ear-splitting volume. Don't let the tunes distract you as you hunt him out.

COMOBOT Although he looks like just any old robot, Comobot defies his mechanical parts — he is totally waterproof and loves to swim.

MAGICAL KINGDOM

Mystical, magical and mysterious, enter this enchanted kingdom and observe the pixie-ish Misfits at play. Their mischievous antics might find them singing and dancing together around the Fairy Flower, the beautiful centrepiece of the fairy habitat.

HUNDEER Travelling to the kingdom, Hundeer has one thing in mind — kidnapping some fairy Misfits to take back to the science lab, where the chief scientist wants to extract their magic. Find Hundeer before he succeeds in his quest.

NOTA A lyrical beast with an angelic singing voice, you might be able to hear Nota as she soothes the Misfits to sleep with lullabies.

CRAW A bit of an outcast in the magical kingdom, Craw is a super-grumpy Misfit who thought he was heading on an alpine adventure but got lost and was rescued by the magic of the fairies.

STANIO Naughty Stanio gets bored easily and is always playing pranks on the other Misfits. He is yet to complete his most ambitious escapade, though, stealing the tairy flower from right under everyone's noses.

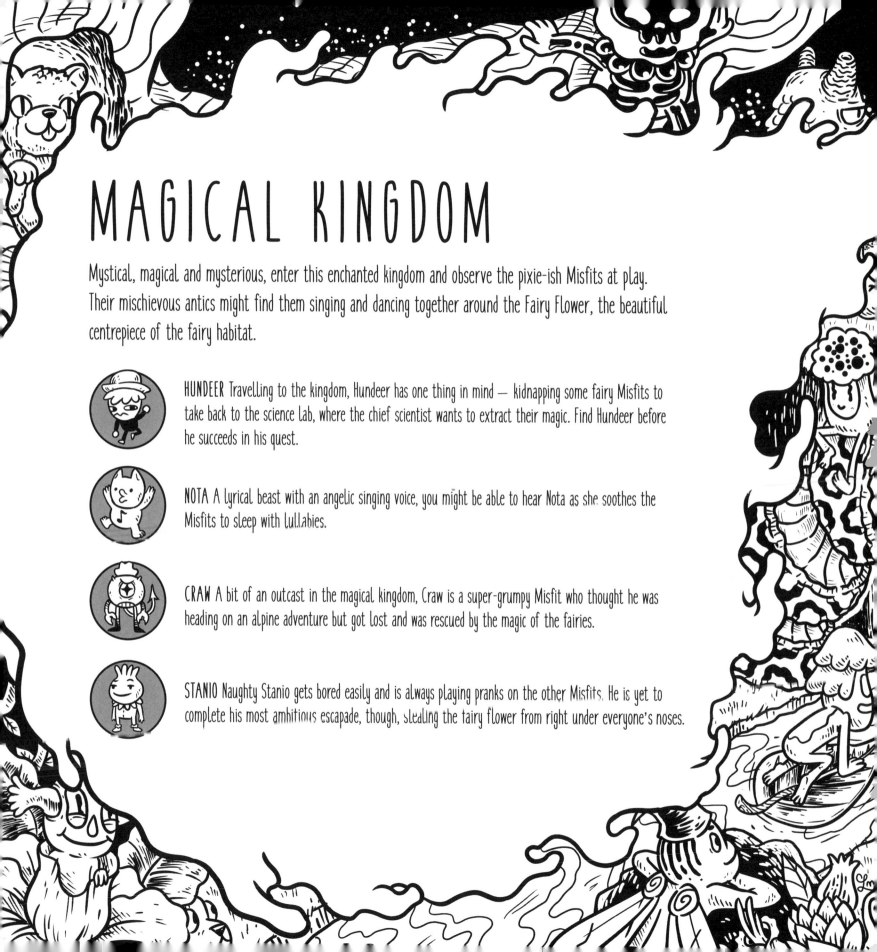

LOST IN THE CITY

This bustling metropolis is a hotchpotch of all things weird and wonderful — tiny shopfronts harbouring big surprises, giant billboards advertising the latest in Misfit technology. It's a feast for the senses, but be careful, before you know it you could be drawn into the buzz and get lost in the city ... FOREVER!

 VOUSNER The sensible one of the Misfit community, Vousner is always on duty, patrolling the streets to make sure that there are no accidents on his watch. Some Misfits find his busybody habits annoying.

 DWAR Famous for sleepwalking through life, Dwar can negotiate the whole city with his eyes closed — even crossing the street poses no problems to this dozing daredevil.

 CREAMO Long days spent hanging around ice-cream parlours and sweet shops are a dream come true for this sweet-toothed fellow.

 POP EYE Eyes quite literally out on stalks, Pop eye is always watching from his perch high above the city. So much so that he has fallen out with Vousner, who feels he is stepping on his surveillance toes.

SCORCHED EARTH

Not much could survive this blazing sun and barren landscape, but these oddities have adapted to their surroundings and are using every advantage they have to evade you. Use the clues below to help pick them out.

ARCHILAR An amateur archaeologist with a special interest in digging up bones, Archilar has dedicated his life to finding a rare skeleton that he thinks will make him famous. Will you find him before he excavates the whole desert?

ROBIN WOOD Poor Robin had a traumatic experience while taking part in a free-flying show and ever since Is a very nervous flyer.

BUD MAN Convinced that his bud head will one day grow into a tree, Bud Man's best friends are all of the plant variety. Companions are few and far between because Bud likes to hang out near the spikiest plants.

MR FLUFFY More cuddly and sensitive than most Misfits, Mr Fluffy seeks out dark nooks and crannies where he won't be picked on. Can you find him and cheer him up before he gets too lonely?

SEWER SEARCH

No one would expect such a selection of oddities to be loitering in this underground network, but dark and dingy corners make this the perfect subterranean hideout for these monstrous Misfits.

MELLOW As laidback as his name suggests, Mellow values his shut-eye above all else and has mastered the art of sleeping with his eyes open. Even the hardest floors make a comfortable bed for this tired terror.

HAIRY HARRY The first giant squid in history to be born with long, thick hair, Harry puts his slime to good use styling his crowning glory and is often found checking his reflection in the closest shiny surface.

ALTO A champion swimmer who loves nothing more than splashing, diving and racing other Misfits, Alto doesn't let the dubious water quality in his sewer hideout put him off his hobby.

GLOVERY Mischievous Misfit Glovery loves jumping out of the waste pipes and scaring her fellow creatures.

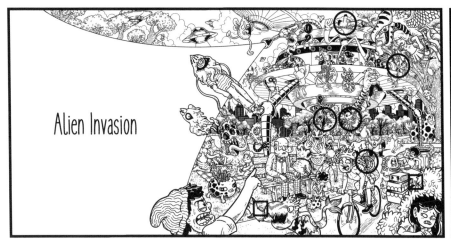

Alien Invasion

Cookie, pencil

Crazy Town

Dice, milk carton, pencil

Food Fight

Dice, ninja star

Time Traveller

Acorn, cookie

Candy Land

Acorn, cookie, dice

Alpine Adventure

Coffee cup, ninja star

Circus

Cookie, dice

Fright Night

Acorn, coffee cup, milk carton

Future City

Cookie, milk carton

Fairground

Astros, ninja star

Science Lab

Coffee cup, ninja star

Super Safari

Acorn, milk carton, pencil

North Pole

Coffee cup, ninja star

Graveyard

Dice, pencil

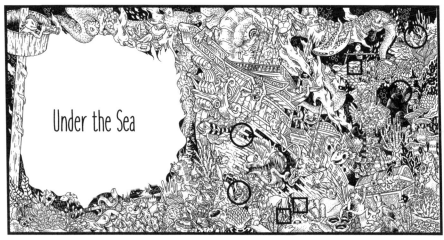

Under the Sea

Acorn, milk carton, pencil

Robot Factory

Coffee cup, cookie

River Rampage

Coffee cup, ninja star

Skate Park

Acorn, milk carton

Forest Hunt

Acorn, pencil

Haunted House

Milk carton, ninja star

Infinity and Beyond

Acorn, cookie, dice

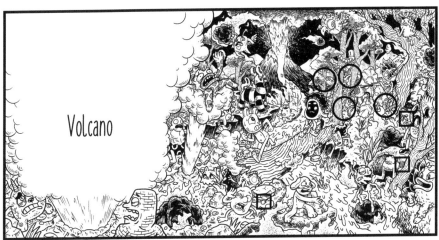

Volcano

Acorn, ninja star, pencil

Rainforest

Cookie, milk carton

Pool Party

Coffee cup, ninja star

Magical Kingdom

Acorn, coffee cup, ninja star

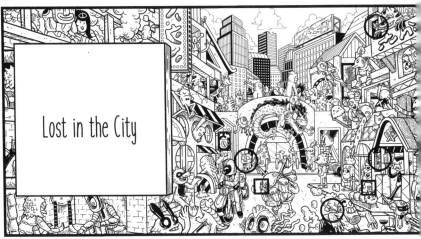

Lost in the City

Dice, pencil

Scorched Earth

Cookie, dice, milk carton

Sewer Search

Coffee cup, pencil

Edited by Jocelyn Norbury
Designed by Derrian Bradder
Cover Design by John Bigwood

First published in Great Britain in 2017 by
LOM ART, an imprint of Michael O'Mara Books Limited,
9 Lion Yard, Tremadoc Road, London SW4 7NQ

W www.mombooks.com
f Michael O'Mara Books
y @OMaraBooks

Copyright © Michael O'Mara Books Limited 2017

A CIP catalogue record for this book is available from the British Library.

ISBN: 978-1-910552-75-9

1 3 5 7 9 10 8 6 4 2

This book was printed in Malta

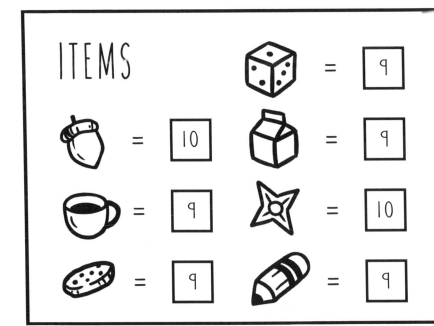

ITEMS

dice = 9
acorn = 10
milk carton = 9
coffee cup = 9
ninja star = 10
cookie = 9
pencil = 9